The Giving Book

Creative Classroom Approaches to Caring, Valuing and Cooperating

by Bob Stanish

photographs by Frank Crocker

Cover by Vanessa Filkins
Copyright © Good Apple, Inc., 1988
ISBN No. 0-86653-459-8
Printing No. 98765432

GOOD APPLE, INC.
BOX 299
CARTHAGE, IL 62321-0299

Table of Contents

Activities

Introduction

The Giving Book is intended to help teachers nurture and develop among students certain attitudes and behaviors that appear to be conducive to growing, learning, developing and becoming. Due to rapid economic and technological changes within our society, family adult time with the child has diminished. The extent of this has impacted on and has altered the role of teaching and learning.

The exercises and activities in this book are not intended to foster a particular set of values, but to encourage the development of values. The exercises and activities in this book are not intended to replace instructional time, but to enhance instructional time. *The Giving Book* promotes caring, valuing, and cooperating and the individual dignity of the child. It is a gentle, loving and usable book of classroom activity ideas and suggestions. It does not contain a model for teaching, learning or doing, but it has the elements of many models. The book was written on the premise that student attitudes and behaviors do affect what is learned, how it is learned and to what extent anything is learned.

The content and processes of this publication come from my own personal concerns and experiences in a classroom. I designed them to meet my requirements and perceptions as I related to and taught children. They have, I believe, carry-over potential into other classrooms.

For the purposes of more fully understanding the three major behaviors and attitudes for which this book addresses, these definitions and explanations are given:

Caring

Caring is viewed as expressing sensitivity towards others and to situations and conditions that affect our behavior and the behavior of others. Caring is also viewed as a willingness to listen, to comprehend, and at times, to act in behalf of, or to provide assistance to others. It is attending to the well being, concerns and feelings of others. Caring is a cluster of behaviors such as sharing, courtesy, tenderness, kindness, empathy, acceptance, responsibility and thoughtfulness. Caring is seen as a necessary element prior to commitment. In order to commit ourselves to anything, we should have first the commitment to care.

Valuing

Valuing is viewed as a commitment to act upon what is valued. The value cherished may be religion or ethics or a philosophy or a belief or the concept of family or work or an organization or education or an expertise or talent. This commitment involves time, effort, and consistent public pronouncements of the value declared. Values are best attained when choices are involved. However, it is not the intent of this book to provide a specific method for value attainment.

Cooperating

Like caring, cooperating is viewed as a cluster of behaviors. These behaviors would include synergy, participating, contributing, collaborating, getting along with others, the ability to resolve conflict, trusting, giving, receiving, negotiating, and coordinating. It is seeking agreement without sacrificing basic value beliefs. As viewed within the framework of a classroom, cooperating is the social ability of working with and getting along with others on a provided task.

The most dominant motivation and reward for most teachers lies in the development and growth of their students. This impact on the lives of students sustains the teaching time and effort made. Today, this is becoming ever so more difficult due to student attitudes about learning, increasing class size, additional responsibilities, additional paperwork and administrative decisions that undermine feelings of competence and efficacy among teachers. It is because of these reasons that the title, *The Giving Book*, is given. It is given to the giving teacher.

I remember not the teacher who assigned the exercise.

I do remember the teacher who cherished and cared for me when I worked the exercise.

I am a by-product of her starlight—her nova.
I am the by-product of all those who have shared their novas with me. I carry their starlight.

And through my burst of starlight is their starlight.

It is within my being. I am because of them.[1]

Amid the exercise pages to follow are statements not unlike the one above. They contain my beliefs and values and my purpose, as I perceive my purpose, for being. And amid the exercise pages are some selected photographs that in a visual sense reflect, for me, the concept of giving.

[1]From *Lessons from the Hearthstone Traveler* by Bob Stanish. Permission granted by Good Apple, Inc.

Activity Index

Page	Activity Title	Caring	Valuing	Cooperating
	Major Focus = ■			
1	Giving	■		■
5	Flowering		■	■
9	Accepting	■		■
11	Cooperative Collage			■
15	The Cooperative Game			■
19	The Essential Self		■	
25	Valuing		■	
33	Perceiving	■		
37	Receiving	■		
39	Viewing	■		
43	Learning for Knowing	■	■	
45	Giving Back	■		
47	Forecasting		■	
49	Mindwebbing		■	
55	Favorites		■	
61	Cooperative Structures			■
65	The Compliment Survey	■		
69	Diamonds, Stars and Butterfly Wings	■		
71	Care Cards	■		
73	Remembering	■		
77	Respect	■		
79	Assembly Line			■
83	Find Someone Who . . .	■		■
87	How is it?	■		
89	Star Power	■	■	■
95	Cooperative Components			■
97	Cooperative Inventions			■

The Giving Activities

**The greater
gifts
cannot be purchased or packaged
or even seen.
They come not from the rational mind
but from the giving heart.**

Giving

List things that can be given but not taken.

caring _____

_____

_____

_____

_____

Of all the giving things you listed, which three things are the most important?

_____

_____

_____

_____

_____

_____

_____

_____

A classroom project in cooperation . . .

The Giving Quilt

- Create quilt squares to expand the meaning of *giving*. Use both words and symbols.

- Determine what words and symbols may be used.

- Cooperate on letters to form words. A message can cover several squares.

- Each person is responsible for one square.

- Hang the quilt on a classroom wall. Before the end of school, give the quilt to a hospital to be hung in a waiting room or give it to a nursing home.

That which is given and not taken is of greater value to self.

Teaching Suggestions

1. Encourage responses like love, friendship, supporting, helping, assisting, rewarding, praising, prizing, respecting, cooperating, sharing, a smile, giving, sympathy or empathy, sincerity, sensitivity, patience, believing, truth, trust, integrity, caring, courage, etc.

   Emphasize that items fitting this category cannot be taken because they must be earned. To be loved, to have friends, to receive support, to receive help or assistance, etc., occurs from effort and not by chance.

2. "The Giving Quilt"

   Allow classroom time for planning and cooperation. Have students use home time for creating the quilt squares.

   Use many of the words generated on page 1 for quilt possibilities.

   Work with the art teacher for a combined effort or with parents. In giving the completed quilt, before the end of a school year, to a deserving group or agency, the essence of giving is consumated.

Flowering —————

> **E**ach life-form is unique unto itself. Never before or ever again will any pattern be repeated. This truth is of great magnitude, for it flows throughout all universal forms.

Teaching Suggestions

This exercise deals with the dangers of peer pressure and conformity.

Prior to doing the next page, consider . . .

- providing a bag of peanuts in shells to your class. Have each student select a peanut for careful study; then have them give you the peanut. Mark each peanut with a code of letters and numbers and on a sheet of paper record the name of the student and the associated code. Place the peanuts into a bag and have students find their peanuts.

  Note: This can be done with a natural form, for example, apples, walnuts, leaves from a single tree, etc.

- Afterwards discuss why is it that the universal structure of all life-forms is uniquely different, yet peer pressure is directed towards conformity?

This is the flower of uniqueness.

- Print your name with a black marker or crayon within the inner circle.

- Use only two colors, yellow and red, to make your flower unique and different from any other flower. Cooperate with all classmates to make this occur.

- Do not use patterns, but do blend the colors together on each petal in a loving way. Use your fingers to blend in a caring way. Pastels or colored chalk are effective.

- Cut your flower from this paper and place it on a bulletin board with other flowers. Negotiate in an open and trusting way with classmates as to the positioning of your flower.

Additional Flowering Suggestions

- List things that the *pressure* in peer pressure is about. Begin with clothes or drugs and compile an extended list. Underscore the items of greatest pressure.

- Any great contributor to the advancement of the human race dealt with conflict with others. Jesus, Ghandi, King, and others encountered conflict because of their refusal to conform to the wishes of others. Compile a list of names of important contributors to the advancement of progress. Select, through discussion, the ten most important and list through investigation the peer pressure they encountered. Then speculate on how our lives would be different if these ten names would have altered their life efforts.

- Role-play ways to deal with the topics of peer pressure.

- Discuss the positive and negative elements of genetic engineering. What are the dangers of cloning?

- Take magnifying glasses and note the differences between single blades of grass.

- List the areas of conformity in our lives. Determine the positive elements of conformity. Determine the negative elements of conformity.

- List all the differences possible in a pair of identical twins.

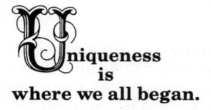 **niqueness**
is
where we all began.

Some of it may get worn through compromise.
Some of it may get tarnished through possession.
Some of it may get wrinkled by money.
Some of it may get shredded by ambition.
Some of it may get broken through conformity.
Some of it may get thinned through security.

If it is unto this earth I come,
it will be from this earth I depart,

Unique.

And if I should stray,
I will
refurbish what has been worn,
polish what has been tarnished,
iron what has been wrinkled,
paste what has been shredded,
mend what has been broken,
and feed what has been thinned.

Accepting

Teaching Suggestions

1. Review the essence of page 10.

2. Sometimes our inabilities to express appreciation and acceptance fully lies in our inabilities to find the words.

   Provide these words for all to see:

Some Positive Attribute Words of Personality and Appearance

artistic	graceful	thoughtful	handsome
bubbly	happy	trusting	neat
caring	helpful	witty	smiling
clever	honest	athletic	stunning
confident	imaginative	attractive	trim
conscientious	intelligent	auburn, brown, blond	well-groomed
considerate	kind	black, red-haired	
courteous	logical	blue, hazel, brown,	or
creative	mature	grey, green-eyed	any words of
dependable	realistic	cute	your choice
forthright	humorous	dimples	that denote a
friendly	serene	distinguished	positive feeling
gentle	sharing	graceful	of self-worth . . .
giving	talented	grinning	

Within all things is a design of infinite beauty.
It takes only a beholder to see.

- You will be given a name
  to be kept a secret.

- By folding a piece of paper
  and cutting geometric designs,
  create a snowflake design.

- Write nine positive attributes
  of the classmate on the design.
  Write the name of the person
  on the back side of the design.

- Give your creation to your
  teacher who will give the
  design to the classmate.

Cooperative Collage

The greatest idea or the greatest thought is always confined to the mind until that confinement is freed. Cooperation has and will always be the freeing agent of ideas.

- Assemble a class into small groups of four to five members.

- Provide each group with . . .
  four half sheets of construction paper of four different colors, some glue and a plain piece of standard-sized paper.

- Provide these instructions:

  1. Without talking or gesturing or communicating in any way, create a collage on a single piece of paper as a group.

  2. Determine, prior to beginning, who in the group will serve as the artist. All other group members will serve as providers.

  3. Each provider will be responsible for providing torn pieces of a single color of construction paper to the artist. Group members try to anticipate what the artist is creating. In doing so, they

tear pieces of construction paper which are offered to the artist. The artist can only take one piece at one time. Once the piece taken is glued, group members discard the unaccepted pieces and tear new ones. The process continues until a picture is completed.

4. The artist will glue single pieces of construction paper to the white paper to create the collage. All four colors of construction paper must be represented in the collage.

5. Approval of the creation may be accomplished by having providers touch gently the shoulder of the artist during the process of creating.

6. All groups must work on a single artistic idea.

Teacher choices of collage construction . . .

- A Human Face of Kindness
- A Loving Creature That Would Appeal to a Child
- A Tree of Happiness
- A Wish for the World

Teaching Suggestions

Key Questions:

1. What did you learn about cooperation?

2. In what ways is approval important to cooperation?

3. In terms of what you learned, how might it be applied . . .

   - to nations?
   - to businesses?
   - to schools?
   - to families?
   - to friendships?

4. In reviewing what you did, which is more important . . .

   - the end product?
   - the making of the product?

Also, discuss the role of support as it applies to cooperative human effort.

Note to teachers: Cooperation requires opportunities to cooperate. Consider doing this exercise again with different collage topics and different artists.

The **Cooperation**
Game

This game consists of three members: one official, one player and one cooperative player.

- The **official** determines a designated space on the grid privately and writes the location on a piece of paper. Locations are determined by numbers and letters. In other words, the first space is 1A, the last space 6G, etc.

- The **player** attempts to locate the designated space by asking five questions. The questions must be worded so that an official's response is either *yes* or *no*.

- The **cooperative player** assists the player in planning a pregame strategy, that is, devising five questions that generate important data. After the last question, a guess is made by the player as to the exact location of the designated space. Once the game begins, there can be no verbal exchanges between the cooperative player and the player. But they can transmit messages through a devised plan of nonverbal messages. These messages should be planned during the pregame planning session.

The player and cooperative player may revise strategies prior to each new game.

The Cooperation Gameboard

	1	2	3	4	5	6
A						
B						
C						
D						
E						
F						
G						

Teaching Suggestions

The key to the game is in the planning session between the player and the cooperative player. Questions developed that ask questions like *Is the designated space between 1A and 6G?* will be more productive than a simple guess. It is very important, however, that the team members make this discovery on their own during the games. Nonverbal messages are important, too. As an observer, the cooperative player will have a different perspective than the player.

Key Questions:

1. How important is communication and planning to human cooperation . . .

   in a marriage?
   at a place of work?
   on an athletic team?

2. How important is questioning to solving problems?

   Give examples of effective questioning in The Cooperation Game.

   Give examples of less effective questioning in The Cooperation Game.

3. How would you account for improved game playing after the first few games? What factors were involved?

4. In what ways can this game be applied to living and problem solving?

Cooperation can best be defined
by what it isn't.

"Where today is the Pequot? Where are the Narragansets, the Mohawks, the Pokanoket, and many other once powerful tribes of our people? They have vanished before the avarice and the oppression of the White Man, as snow before a summer sun."

Tecumseh, Shawnee Chief

The **Essential** ─────────
Self

Create a design of self by following
these directions:

- On page 20, select one of three designs that would best describe
  you. Use a ruler and draw the design on the grid (page 22).

- Within the outer design, select one of two inner designs that would
  best describe you. Use a ruler and draw this design within the
  outer design.

- Within the inner design, draw either the one-cube design or the
  two-cube design relating to your sex.

  - On page 21, follow the directions of the color chart to further
    explain yourself.

    And finally . . .

- Give your pattern a secret code because other classmates will
  attempt to identify the design of your essential self with you.

  Try to accurately design your symbol with what you know about
  yourself. Do not allow anyone to see you prepare your design.

The Essential Self

The Designs

The Outer Design (select one):

pentagon   octagon   hexagon

outgoing   reserved   in-between

The Inner Design (select one):

pyramid   inverted pyramid

practical   imaginative

The Core (select one):

one cube   two cubes

boy   girl

The Essential Self

The Coloring Chart

Outer Design Colors (select one):

    yellow   ● preference for many friends
    orange   ● preference for some friends
    red   ● preference for one or two good friends

Inner Design Colors (select one):

    blue   ● a good follower
    green   ● a good leader
    blue-green ● sometimes a leader; some-times a follower

Spaces Between Designs (select one):

    light blue   ● serious minded
    yellow-green ● happy-go-lucky

Example

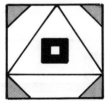

light blue or
yellow-green

Inner core cubes are black for boys.

Inner core cubes for girls are black with a smaller white cube.

The Essential Self

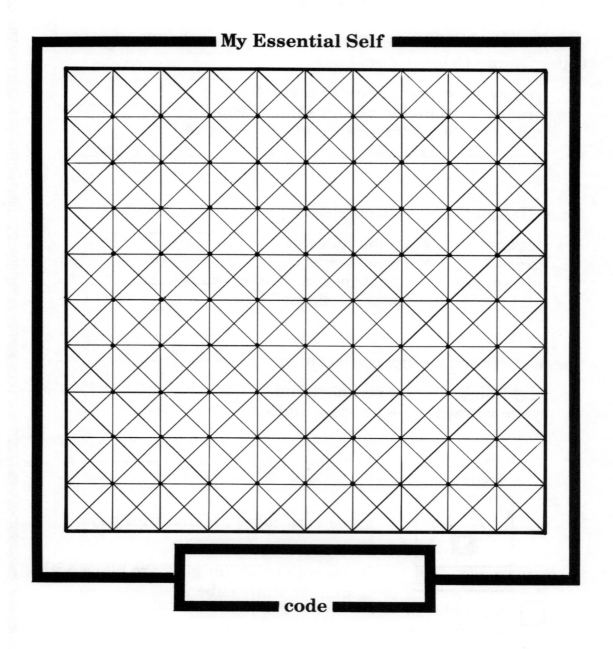

My Essential Self

code

Scoring Sheet

Code	Who I think it is . . .	

Place a ✔ in a box for
each correct guess.

Teaching Suggestions on
The Essential Self

The key element is . . . **Are we what others perceive us to be?**

- Encourage students to work in isolated areas on the development of their designs.

  In many instances, you will be presented with a difficult-to-choose design. Insist that students make a choice.

- Have students give to you the designs upon completion. Each design should have a code assigned by the student or yourself.

- Have your class wait outside the classroom while you place the designs on a wall.

- Upon entering the classroom they are to determine what belongs to whom. Use the Scoring Sheet for this purpose.

- Opportunities for an interesting group discussion:

  1. Are we really what others perceive us to be?
  2. Are we accurate in making judgments about others?
  3. How well do we really know ourselves?
  4. In what ways can one alter his/her design of the essential self?

Valuing

Valuing is the art of confirming publically and to our inner selves what is important—what is of value. It is the sum total of who we are.

The exercises on the next several pages consist of choices. Some of the choices will be difficult. It is important to confirm and announce what aspects of living are the most important to who we are and what we believe. We become more positive and more in control of our lives when we have an understanding as to what is important to us. The purpose of this section is not to debate, but to announce. Acceptance of all attitudes and beliefs is recommended.

The *vertical rating pole* is a device in which a polarity of opinions may be placed. We can see the extent of our attitudes and opinions in using it. It will appear frequently in the exercises to follow.

- With each exercise, students are to:

    1. provide written choices.

    2. anticipate how their choices will compare with the choices listed by classmates.

    3. provide justification for choices made.

National Concerns

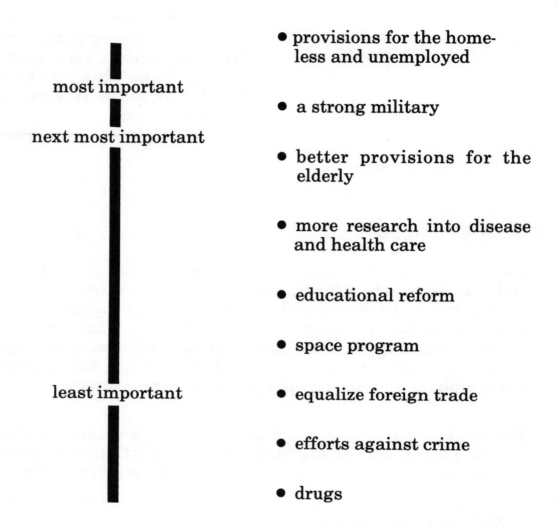

most important

next most important

least important

- provisions for the homeless and unemployed

- a strong military

- better provisions for the elderly

- more research into disease and health care

- educational reform

- space program

- equalize foreign trade

- efforts against crime

- drugs

Suppose you could direct most of the nation's monies and efforts to only two major concerns. Write your choices across the top portion of the vertical rating pole. Write the least important of the choices at the bottom end of the pole. Be prepared to justify your choices.

- I will probably be in the majority opinion. ☐
- I will probably be in the minority opinion. ☐

Personality

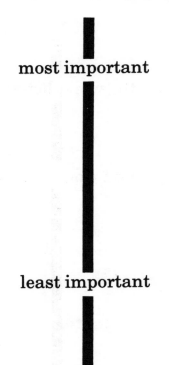

- outgoing
- courageous
- intelligent
- imaginative
- leadership
- morality
- responsible
- happy-go-lucky
- sincere
- shrewd
- practical
- venturesome

most important

least important

Write the two most important human personality traits of those listed under most important.

Write the two least important human personality traits of those listed under least important.

- My opinions are probably different from most of my classmates. ☐

- My opinions are probably similar to most of my classmates. ☐

Behaviors

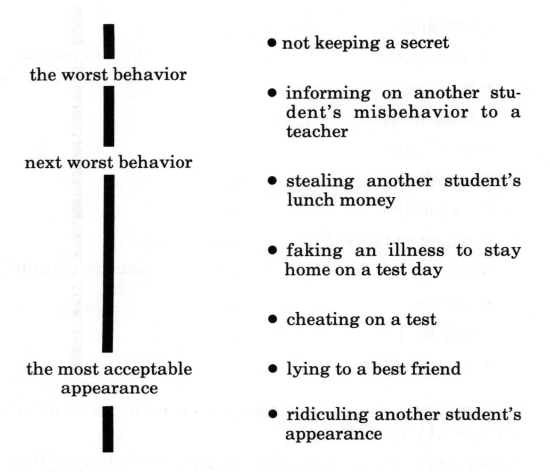

the worst behavior

next worst behavior

the most acceptable
appearance

- not keeping a secret

- informing on another student's misbehavior to a teacher

- stealing another student's lunch money

- faking an illness to stay home on a test day

- cheating on a test

- lying to a best friend

- ridiculing another student's appearance

Select three behaviors from the list and place them on the vertical rating pole.

Try to predict how your selections will compare with your classmates' choices.

- My choices will be fairly similar.   ☐
- My choices will be different.   ☐

Future Desires

Place these future desires in order by writing them across the vertical rating pole. In other words, the desire of greatest importance is to be written at the very top of the pole, the desire deemed next in importance, second, etc.

most important

- interesting job
- family
- college education
- popularity
- leadership
- financial security
- respect of peers
- recreational pursuits and interests

- My arrangement will probably be similar ☐ to most of my classmates.

- My arrangement will probably not be ☐ similar to most of my classmates.

29

Nonschool Time

Indicate how you spend most of your away-from-school time. Write across the vertical rating pole topics that fit.

The most popular choice of my class will probably be _____ .

- television

- radio or stereo

- reading

- board games

- studying

- chores

- part-time work

- organized sports

- organizations

- hobby

- play

- telephoning

- relaxing

- _____

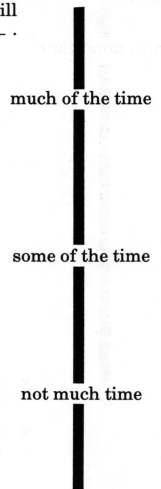

much of the time

some of the time

not much time

Developing

Indicate which of the human behaviors listed are of the greatest value towards the development and continuance of the human species.

My opinion, in comparison to those of my classmates, will probably be . . .

very different from others	☐
somewhat different from others	☐
somewhat similar to others	☐
very similar to others	☐

- sharing

- giving

- caring

- loving

- trusting

- respecting

- cooperating

most important

next most important

third most important

Teaching Suggestions on Valuing

- The purpose of these exercises is to provide opportunity to consider and express opinions on some basic elements affecting human conditions and aspirations.

  It is important that acceptance of all opinions is encouraged. The important thing is having an opinion and a belief. These are the intrinsic possessions—far more important than material possessions.

- The vertical rating pole offers a visual benefit to viewing values, attitudes and beliefs. Use this device in expanding the concept of valuing and viewing things of real importance.

- Projecting and forecasting how one's opinion will compare with the opinions of others is intended to nurture strength of conviction and confidence in one's own thinking. Placing contingencies on debate within these exercises will support this position.

Sharing

In sharing, I say, I am but me.
Receive,
reject,
or take portions of me,
I am but a river
that flows to the sea.

Perceiving

Circle the fish among the fish that
is most like you and explain why.

Teaching Suggestions on Perceiving

- Allow for self-interpretation and analysis. The responses will reflect some interesting aspects of how students perceive themselves in relationship to a group or class.

    The most common interpretations would include . . . The lead fish as a leader; the fish with the black fins as following the group but maintaining its own traits or individuality; fish in the group as followers and the fish in the lower left as unique and a contrariant or imaginative.

- Look at the written responses as an avenue for discovering more information about your students and how they perceive themselves.

    This exercise is not intended to be used as a basis for class or group discussion.

- If this exercise is utilized early in the school year, do it again late in the school year and compare results from individual students.

Earth and sky
are nurtured by the warmth
of the giving sun.

And from this nurturing,
conditions appear.

And from these conditions,
a seed appears.

The seed, if nurtured well,
may bud
its being and the essence of its growth
upon the receiving earth.

The nurture of warmth bestowed
by one giving teacher
may bud forth a child of such importance
and that earth, sky, the giving sun
and all living things will rejoyce
and receive benefit from this
single act of giving.

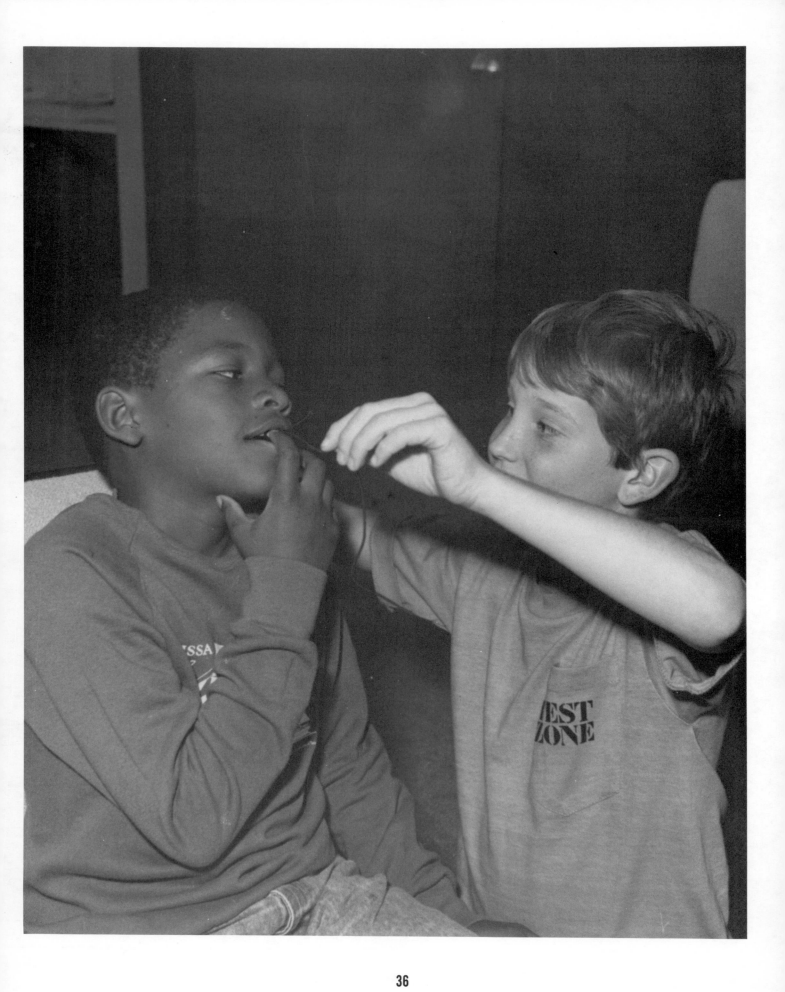

Receiving ────────

Circle seven verbs or action words that effectively describe the person mentioned below.

_____

accepts	composes	excites	laughs
advises	confers	experiments	learns
assists	congratulates	explains	organizes
attracts	considers	feels	participates
befriends	corrects	fixes	plays
builds	creates	gives	pleases
calms	defines	helps	praises
cares	delivers	imagines	receives
challenges	demonstrates	improves	socializes
cheers	diagnoses	invents	studies
clarifies	earns	investigates	supports
collects	endures	jokes	succeeds
comforts	enjoys	judges	tries
compliments	excels	knows	values

Teaching Suggestions

This exercise is for focusing on one youngster at a time. It is an exercise of giving and receiving. Name the student for focus. Have all other students cite seven verbs that best describe the individual as they know the individual.

All the cited verbs are then given to the student. The student receiving the verbs then determines the most popular words assigned to him or her. At some later time in the day, the student announces the count of the seven most popular verbs.

At periodic intervals, repeat this exercise so that all students will have an opportunity to have the focus of receiving.

Key Questions:

1. Are the perceptions of self similar to group perceptions of self?

2. Is positive information or feedback difficult to receive?

3. Is there a more positive feeling of self because of this exercise?

4. Which is more beneficial—negative reinforcement or positive reinforcement?

   Note: The answers to questions 2 through 4 are obvious, but the questions and answers are important discussion topics in any group.

Viewing

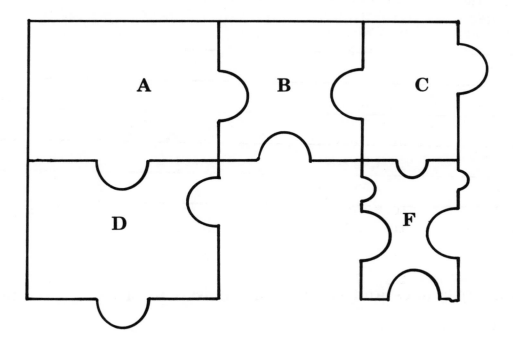

A = Most important piece to begin play.

B = Dependent on A; medium difficulty to locate. Does not offer assistance in finding E.

C = Important border piece; offers assistance in finding F.

D = An important piece but offers little in its pattern in locating other pieces.

E = This piece is missing.

F = Very obliging piece that offers assistance to surrounding pieces.

Viewing

1. In classroom group or committee work, I am most like piece ____ because

   _____

   _____

   _____

   _____

   _____

   _____

2. In group games and sports, I am most like piece ____ because

   _____

   _____

   _____

   _____

   _____

   _____

   _____

3. In school, _____ resembles piece A.
   (name of student)

4. In school, _____ resembles piece F.
   (name of student)

Respond to this exercise and compare your reactions to those of a classmate or two.

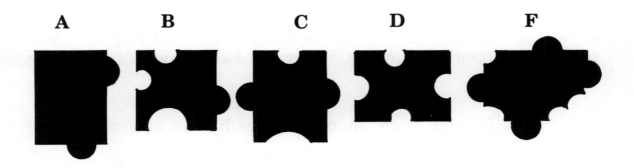

A   B   C   D   F

1. If I had to be a jigsaw puzzle piece, I'd choose piece_____ because

_____

_____

_____

_____

2. One piece I wouldn't want to be connected to is piece_____ because

_____

_____

_____

_____

Teaching Suggestions on Viewing

- This exercise is for gaining additional information about students. It will also provide interesting insight into how students perceive other students.

- The concept of a jigsaw puzzle relating to human behavior draws upon metaphorical thinking. Follow this exercise with questioning like:

    1. In what ways are our feelings like an automobile tire?

    2. In what ways are our successes like a rippling pond?

    3. In what ways are our failures like rolling thunder?

    4. In what ways are we like a seashell?

    5. In what ways are we like a gliding eagle?

    6. In what ways are we like a rolling stone?

There are no wrong answers to the questions above. It is the explanation given that is of importance. Look for insight and association. For example, some possible responses to item 1, might include: *Our feelings can be inflated or deflated like a tire . . . Our feelings can be punctured much like a tire . . . Like a tire, our feelings may require something like springs or reflection to recover. Sometimes feelings, like tires, need to be realigned.*

Learning for ——
Knowing

Knowing how a person thinks and feels is a beginning dimension. A far greater dimension is knowing how thoughts and feelings became. True human closeness has a proximity to the becoming process.

The purpose of this exercise is to acquaint students about students.

Teaching Suggestions

- In private and without notice, provide the exercise sheets to a selected student.

- At some future time, read both the statements and responses to the total class.

- The class objective is to determine what student was selected based upon the responses heard.

- The name of the suspected student is written on paper and a tally taken of the name selection.

- After the tally is taken, the name is revealed.

- This exercise is repeated with different names throughout the school year.

Who am I?

1. Happiness to me means

_____

_____

_____

_____

2. When I am really bored, I sometimes daydream about

_____

_____

_____

_____

3. Something about me that would surprise most people is

_____

_____

_____

_____

4. Someday I would like to

_____

_____

_____

_____

Giving Back

As teachers it is important to receive feedback or some acknowledgement of effort.

By enormous proportions, the best assessment of effort is by the ones that receive your effort—your students.

This exercise is for you. Select a day in which you need some positive reinforcement.

Teaching Suggestions

- Duplicate copies of page 46 for all students.

- They are to select both behaviors and traits that would best describe you. The behaviors and traits are color-coded and the four colors selected are to be placed on the diamond.

- For a super effect, paste to cardboard and place a pencil in the center of the diamond for an axle. Have everyone spin their diamond at the same time. See what predominant colors appear.

    This exercise can give some very interesting perceptions of you as both an individual and a teacher.

Dark Lined Stripes

Choose the two behaviors and colors that would best describe your teacher.

- blue for giving
- red for caring
- yellow for trying
- green for patience
- orange for sharing

Lighter Lined Stripes

Choose the two traits and colors that would best describe your teacher.

- blue for imaginative
- red for calm
- purple for logical
- yellow for humorous
- pink for warmhearted

Alternate the two colors so that stripes appear on sides A and D.

Alternate the two colors on lines B and C.

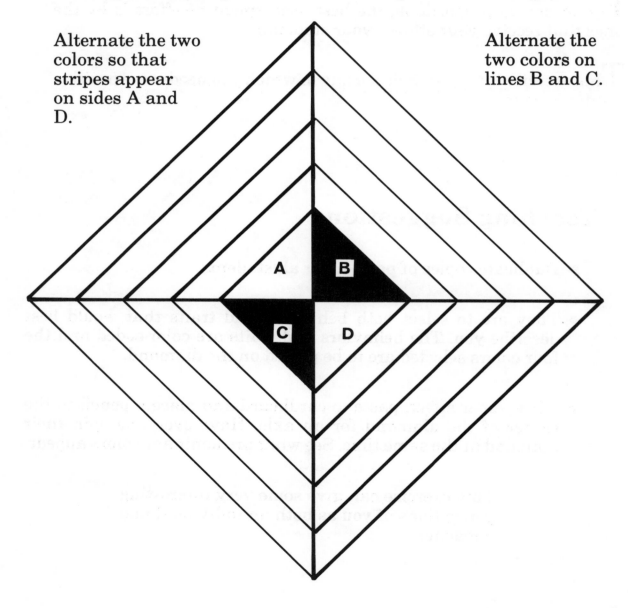

Forecasting

Wishing is a preliminary preamble to establishing goals.

Teaching Suggestions

- Assign as a weekend assignment.

- Provide the same size and color of construction paper to all students.

- When students arrive with their collages, collect them facedown so that secrecy of collages prevails.

- When students are out of the room, mount the collages on a wall and mark a number on each for identification.

- Encourage students to attempt to identify on paper what collage belongs to whom.

- Determine who was able to identify the most collages. Afterwards provide time for each student to explain his own collage.

A Collage of My Future Self

- Using old magazines, paste together a collage of your future self.

- Consider using pictures of things that would require purchasing.

- Consider using pictures that would show use of leisure and fun time.

- Consider using pictures in which an occupation of your future self can be seen.

- Consider using pictures that would symbolize highlights of your future self.

- Do not write your name on your collage. See how many classmates can identify your collage with you.

Mindwebbing———

No more is the day that a teacher is just a teacher. Counselor, mentor, and at times—substitute parent.

This activity consists of four pages. The pages are to be joined to show the connection of school, leisure, and future aspirations of students. Follow these procedures:

- Duplicate all four pages for all students.

- Cut along the thin-line border and connect the four pages on the reverse sides with clear tape.

- The shaded square is for a school photograph or recent photograph of the student. Let each student provide his own photograph. The pages can be easily aligned by using the shaded photograph square areas. Page 52 would be in the upper left, page 53 in the upper right, page 54 in the lower left and page 55 in the lower right of the poster-sized sheet.

- Consider using the Mindwebbing posters on walls for peer interest and information.

  Consider sharing the posters with parents and as a basis for conference meetings.

Teaching Suggestions

- Add more dimensions to this exercise if desired.

  For example, consider a color-coding with light-colored markers or highlighters over the written words of students. Use something like yellow for those rectangles that were easy, light green or pink for the rectangles that required more thought. This would indicate to you those areas of decisiveness and areas of tentativeness.

- Consider joining areas of common interest between posters with yarn to show the networking of common bonds.

- Consider establishing a classroom corner for a weekly highlight of an individual student. Use an individual poster and have that student bring to class material possessions that would dramatize some of the information on the poster.

- Consider having each student present his/her poster so that opportunity for embellishment and detail can be provided.

- As a class, discuss how often leisure interests, school interests and future desires are related.

- Discuss how a webbing strategy like the one in this exercise could be modified and changed to accommodate book reports and other assignments.

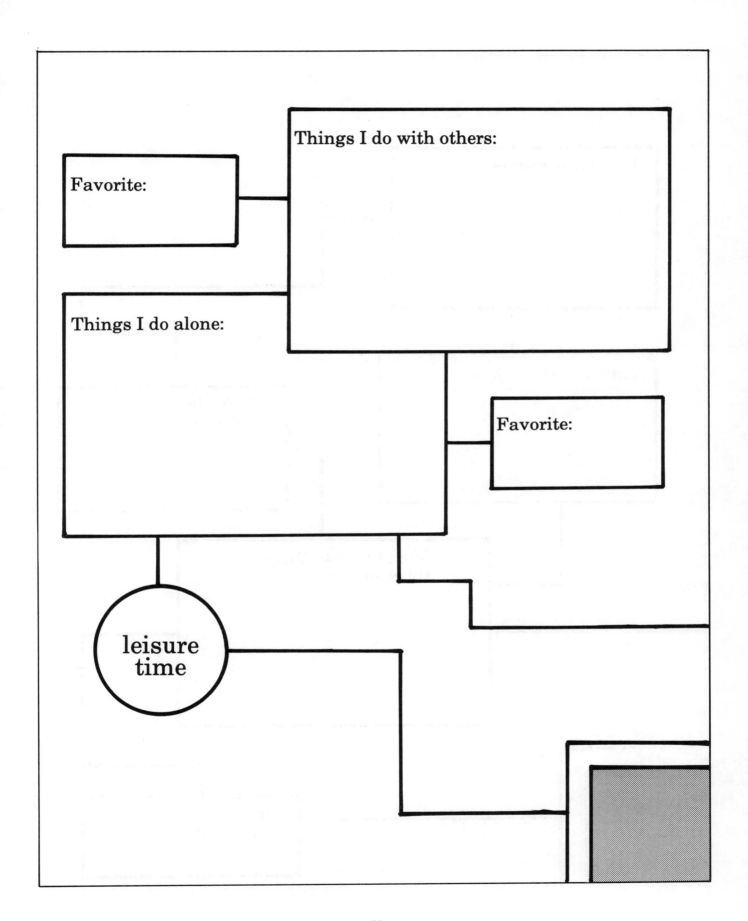

Favorite:

Things I do with others:

Things I do alone:

Favorite:

leisure
time

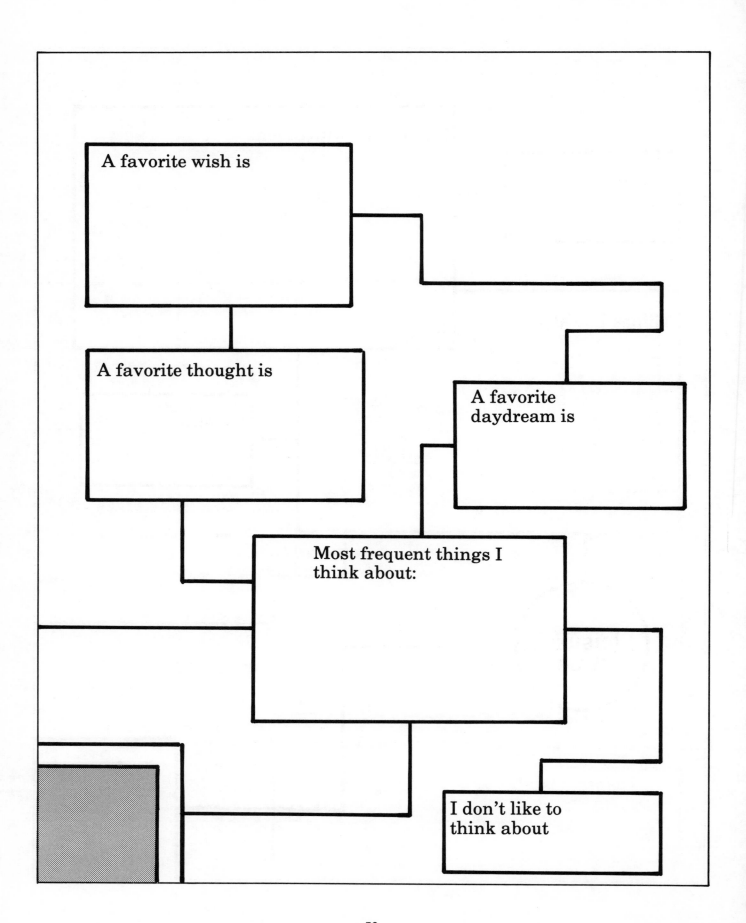

A favorite wish is

A favorite thought is

A favorite daydream is

Most frequent things I think about:

I don't like to think about

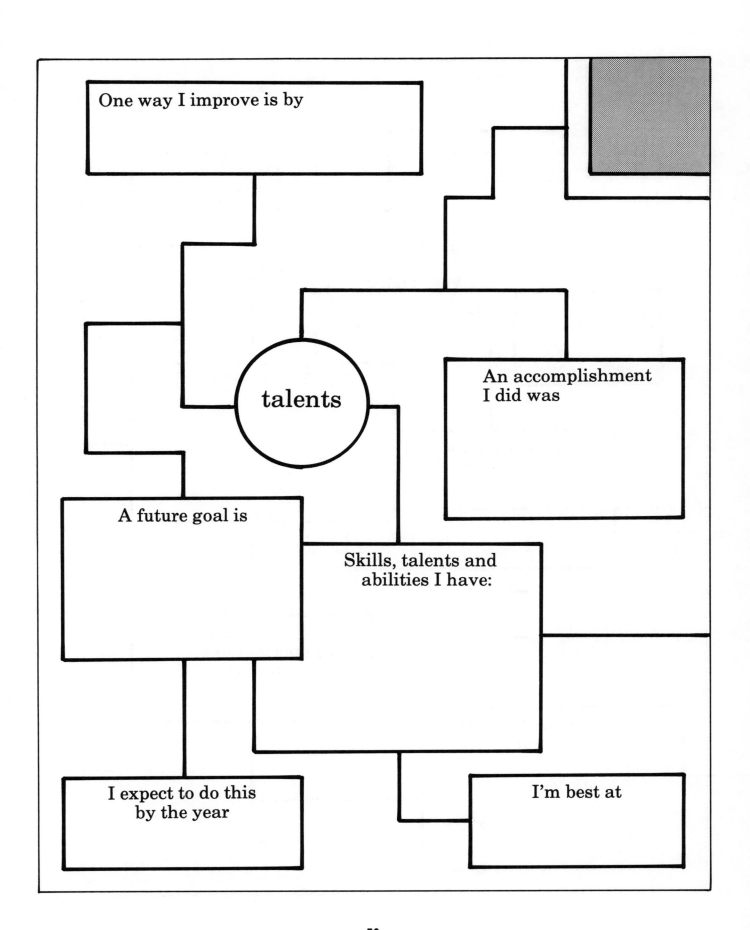

One way I improve is by

talents

An accomplishment
I did was

A future goal is

Skills, talents and
abilities I have:

I expect to do this
by the year

I'm best at

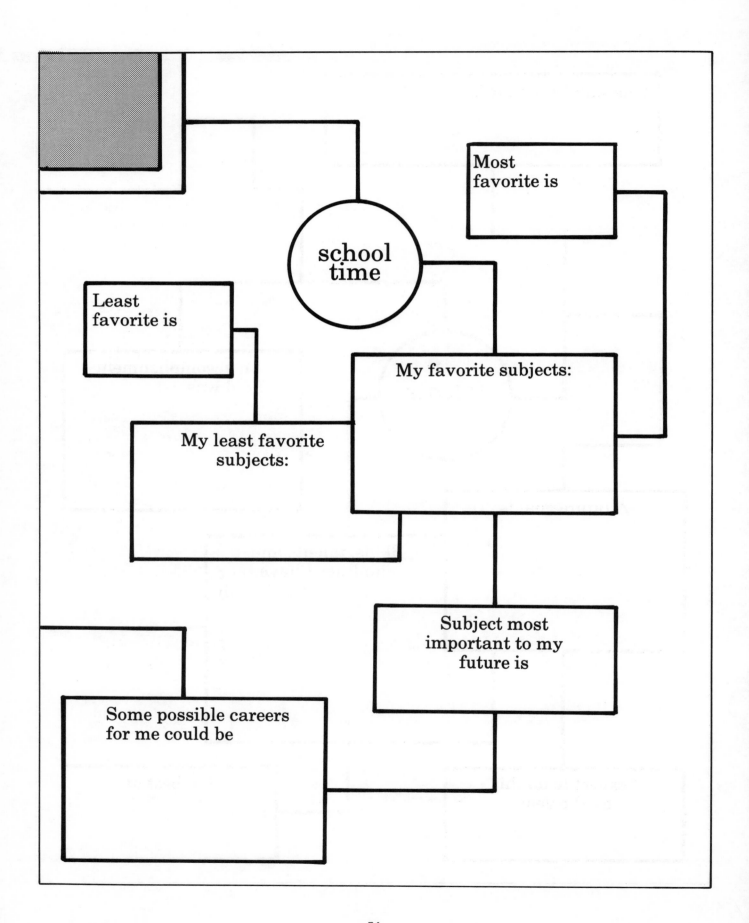

school
time

Most
favorite is

Least
favorite is

My favorite subjects:

My least favorite
subjects:

Subject most
important to my
future is

Some possible careers
for me could be

Favorites

Acceptance begins by knowing.

Teaching Suggestions

- One student per week is selected.

- The student selected will keep his or her identity secret until the last school day in the week at a time provided by the teacher.

- It is recommended that the teacher fills out response sheets to avoid handwriting clues that may be provided by the selected student.

- The completed response sheet is then placed on a bulletin board early in the week for all students to read and study.

- After the student is identified, conduct a brief public interview of that student by using a few questions selected from page 58.

A List of Favorites

Who am I?

1. My favorite indoor thing is _____

2. My favorite outdoor thing is _____

3. My favorite radio station is _____

4. My favorite color is _____

5. My favorite ice-cream flavor is _____

6. My favorite snack is _____

7. My favorite quick food item is _____

8. My favorite board game is _____

9. My favorite song is _____

10. My favorite TV show is _____

11. My favorite school subject is _____

12. My favorite machine is _____

13. My favorite bedtime hour is _____

14. My favorite famous personality is _____

15. My favorite toothpaste is _____

16. My favorite pizza topping is _____

17. My favorite comic strip is _____

18. My favorite book is _____

19. My favorite desire is _____

20. My favorite daydream is _____

21. My favorite store is _____

22. My favorite souvenir or keepsake is _____

23. My favorite breakfast food is _____

24. My favorite home-cooked meal is _____

25. My favorite out-of-town place to visit is _____

26. My favorite wish is _____

27. My favorite television star is _____

28. My favorite flavor is _____

29. My favorite "stay at home" activity is _____

30. My favorite animal at the zoo is _____

31. My favorite pocket or purse item is _____

32. My favorite magazine or comic book is _____

33. My favorite item in the refrigerator is _____

34. My favorite way to travel is _____

Provocative Questions on *Favorites*

1. Which of your favorites would you be most willing to give up? Which would be the most difficult to give up?

2. Which five favorites will most likely change five years from now?

3. Which favorite is the oldest? Which favorite is the most recent?

4. Which favorite is the most repeated and occurring favorite?

5. Which favorites should have been on the list?

6. Which favorite took the most time in responding? Which favorite took the least time in responding?

7. Which favorite would be the most different from other classmates?

8. Which favorite would most likely continue the rest of your life?

9. Which favorite deserves a greater explanation?

10. Which favorite is the most exciting? Which favorite is the least exciting?

11. Which favorite is the most time-consuming?

12. Which favorite is being threatened by replacement and why?

If the greater value is given the score,
then value the score.

If the greater value is intrinsic,
then value the child.

There is, I think,
a far greater value
in
teaching the intrinsic desire to learn
than in
teaching to achieve a score.

If the desire to learn is in its place,
then achievement will find its place.

Cooperative Structures

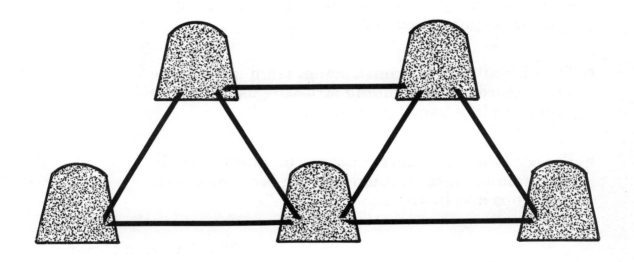

- By taking sugary gumdrops and toothpicks and creating triangles, sturdy structures can be built. Connect one triangle to another triangle to another, etc.

- Follow the rules on the next page for an interesting experiment on small group cooperation.

Rules for
Cooperative Structures

The Construction Team:

- A small group of three to four students will create a free-standing structure by creating triangles made from gumdrops and toothpicks.

- The objective of the construction team is to create a tall, sturdy, free-standing structure using all the gumdrops in a bag of gumdrops.

- The construction team cannot speak. Ideas can only be communicated through giving and receiving gumdrops and toothpicks.

The Observing Team:

- An observing team of three to four students will silently observe the construction team.

- They will look for examples of cooperation, shared leadership, individual leadership and sharing.

- Upon completion of the construction, the observation team will meet and discuss their observations, then share their observations with the entire class.

> **Cooperation is something to be learned. What can be learned can be taught.**

Teaching Suggestions

- Use this opportunity to

  . . . team four leaders into a single construction team group.

  . . . team four nonleaders into a single construction team group.

  Observe what happens.

- Ask all students to list the attributes of cooperation using *ing* words. Examples: *giving, sharing, receiving, anticipating, providing, supporting,* etc.

- If inclined, provide the observation sheet to the observing team for gathering data.

- Ask students to imagine engineering projects of great dimension like the Panama Canal, the Eiffel Tower, The Great Wall of China, the Gateway Arch in St. Louis and to list what kinds of cooperation would have been required from what kinds of people? (Builders, workers, residents living in the area, governments, architects, financial contributors, etc.)

Observation Sheet for Cooperative Structures

Names

Who did most of the building?	
Who did most of the providing?	
Who did most of the cooperating?	
Who gave most of the direction?	
Who engaged in the greatest variety of tasks?	
Who gave the most positive support?	

The Compliment Survey

Fill in the blanks with the names of classmates.

1. A great helper is ——————————————— .

2. ——————————————— always seems to have good advice.

3. Someone I can really depend on is ——————————— .

4. ——————————————— is a good problem solver.

5. I really trust ——————————————————— .

6. ——————————————— really has a nice smile.

The Compliment Survey

7. Someone who shares is _____ .

8. _____ has a nice personality.

9. A great sense of humor has _____ .

10. _____ is both sincere and kind.

11. I like _____'s thoughtfulness.

12. _____ is highly imaginative.

13. A very caring person is _____ .

14. _____ is a very happy person.

The three people whose names appeared most on my survey were:

_____

_____

_____

Teaching Suggestions

The purpose of this activity is to both identify and establish student role models.

By highlighting the most desirable of human behaviors, it is anticipated that premiums in these behaviors will be received—received and duplicated in the behaviors of others.

The data received from the survey should be shared with all students. Reinforcing desirable behavior promotes desirable behavior.

The very nature of this survey says that you, as a teacher, place a high priority on trust, dependability, sharing, caring, giving, sincerity, and kindness in a classroom.

- Use the format on the next page for listing the high scorers from the survey. Place the format on the bulletin board.

- Repeat this exercise in two months to see if peer perceptions are the same.

- Use some of the data received in regularly scheduled parent conferences.

Results of The Compliment Survey

Names

Helping	
Good Advice	
Dependable	
Good Problem Solver	
Trusting	
Smiling	
Sharing	
Personality	
Sense of Humor	
Sincere and Kind	
Thoughtfulness	
Imaginative	
Caring	
Happy	

Most frequently
mentioned names
on survey:

1. _____

2. _____

3. _____

Diamonds, Stars and Butterfly Wings —

The purpose of this exercise is to provide a springboard for discussing some of the important elements in becoming. Allow your imagination to extend it into realms of softness and beauty.

Student Directions

- Inside the design is a six-pointed star. Color the star the color of your birthstone, except for the centered diamond.

- Color the center diamond the color of hope.

- At the points of the star are butterfly wings. Color the wings the color of faith.

- There are six diamonds that touch each wing. Color these diamonds the color of trust.

- And within these designs are background patterns. Color these patterns the color of charity.

    When you see these colors and shapes that extend beyond and within the color of your birthstone, remind yourself that a life of hope, faith, trust, and charity can be with you—if you make it so.

Diamonds, Stars and Butterfly Wings

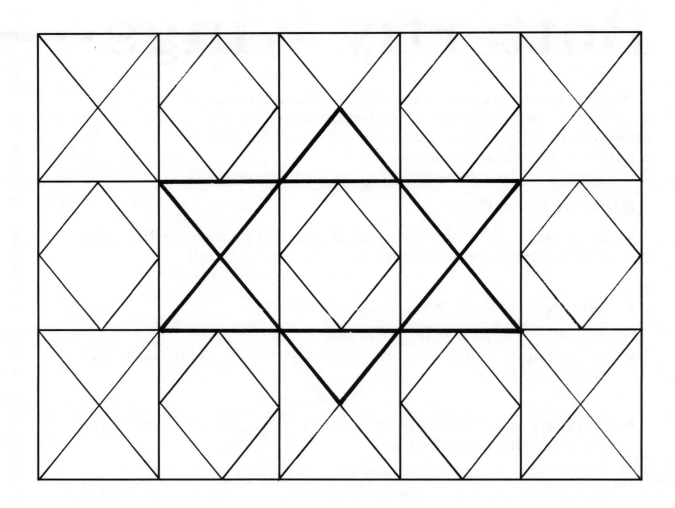

Care Cards

There are greeting cards, birthday cards, happy holiday cards, get well cards and many other kinds of cards.

There are no "I care" cards.

- **Create a Care Card.**

    - Determine something you care about.

    - Determine what kind of an illustration or image or collage that would be related to your subject of caring.

    - Determine what kind of inside statement or poem would be appropriate.

    - Fold a regular-sized piece of white construction paper into a care card.

    - Design the card by placing images and statements on it.

    - Give the card, if possible, to the object of your caring.

Teaching Suggestions on Care Cards

- Begin by group brainstorming things that are the subject of caring. Phrase the question with: "What are some things to care about?" or "What's worth caring about?"

  When or if student ideation is stymied, interject questions like, "What do physicians care about? What do environmentalists care about? What do artists care about? What do musicians care about? What do engineers care about?" Try to gain a broad overview of what is important enough to warrant caring.

- Have a classroom discussion on how some areas of caring for many people determine what they do. For example, many teachers teach because they care about children. Many physicians enter medicine because they care about healing. Many people become associated with nurseries because they care about plants.

- Refer to these areas of real caring as value areas. A person with values is a person who is willing to act upon and defend his views on the areas he really cares about.

- Proceed to the Care Cards.

Remembering————

Responsibility is enhanced by remembering the small thoughtful kinds of things and the major important kinds of things.

The purpose of this activity is to demonstrate that creative thinking and doing can enhance our responsibility for self.

General Overview

Students are to create unique bookmarks to be placed on the beginning page of a textbook homework assignment. By adding embellishment to a simple design, the visual encounter will help stimulate their memory to do the assignment.

Materials Needed

2 copies per student of the **Assignment Reminder Pattern.**

manila folder or poster type cardboard

classroom boxes of scrap fabric

cotton balls

scissors, glue, crayons, colored markers

Optional: needles and thread

Assignment Reminder Pattern

Assignment
Reminder

Beginning page
view of the
Assignment Reminder

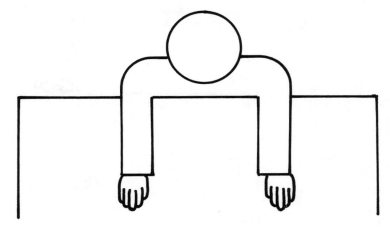

Student Directions

- Paste one pattern to a
piece of poster board.
Cut the pattern and poster board with scissors. Cut along the arm
and hand lines so that the effect above is shown.
Paste the other pattern (this will represent the back of the **Assignment Reminder**) to the first pattern.

- Add a face with a smile to the front. Add some cotton for hair,
mustache or beard.

- Add some clothes, using fabric scraps, with glue or sew them on-
to the pattern. Don't forget the back of the **Assignment Reminder**
for clothes and hair, too!

- Make your design as unique, clever, and original as you can.

- Decide on which textbook you will use the **Assignment Reminder**
and see if remembering to do assignments improves.

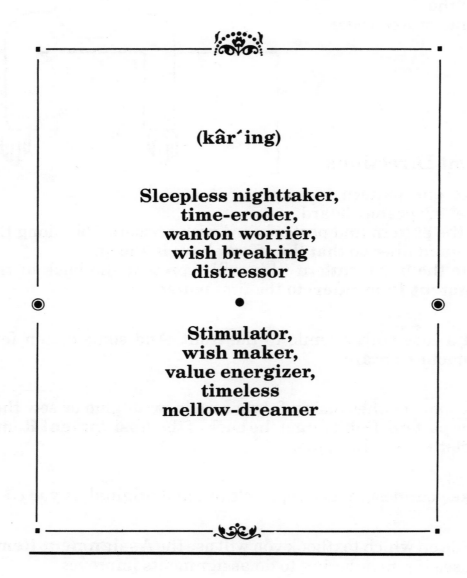

(kâr´ing)

**Sleepless nighttaker,
time-eroder,
wanton worrier,
wish breaking
distressor**

●

**Stimulator,
wish maker,
value energizer,
timeless
mellow-dreamer**

Respect—————

---
re • spect (rĭ-spĕkt´)

To feel or show esteem for; to honor.

List three nonrelated persons
who deserve your respect.

1. I respect _____

   because _____

   _____

   _____

   _____

2. I respect _____

   because _____

   _____

   _____

   _____

3. I respect _____

   because _____

   _____

   _____

   _____

Imagine the three names you listed were suddenly merged into one personality of respect. What human qualities would this special person have? Write them across the illustration.

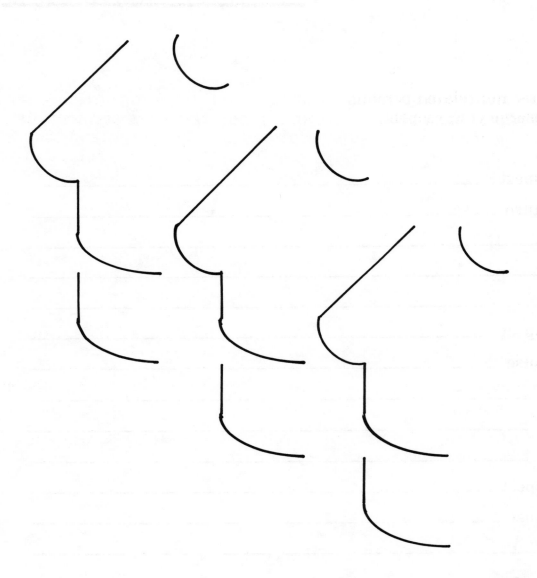

Assembly Line——

an exercise in cooperation

Overview

Groups of three students are given an incomplete drawing on a single piece of paper. Each student within a group extends a segment of the drawing towards the center of the paper. Without talking but with nonverbal communication, an attempt is made to synthesize the three fragmented incomplete drawings into a single, recognizable image.

Teaching Suggestions

- Provide the problem overview.

- After completion, have students in groups discuss . . .

    - How important is knowing what other group members were doing during the drawing process?

    - How important was it to alter one's original intent in order to accommodate a group project?

    - With what kinds of adult situations would these kinds of behaviors be the same?

Each person takes an incomplete drawing and extends it towards the center. The objective is to create, among you, a recognizable drawing. No clouds allowed or talking during this exercise.

What
a child
feels about self
determines
what and to what degree
anything is learned.

May
every child
be given
the essence
and dignity of self
by one
caring and giving
teacher.

For it is of this sowing
that the
harvest comes.

Find Someone Who . . .

One of the truly magnificent things about knowledge is that it can be shared.

Teaching Suggestions

- There are three different exercises to this activity. Use them periodically.

- Stress the importance of gaining knowledge by meeting and knowing people. One of the things that comes with the knowing is sharing. It is through these encounters that we extend our boundaries of knowing.

- Students are to interview students and adults to find answers to the exercise questions.

- Afterwards, talk in terms of primary sources of information; talk in terms of the importance of oral history and talk about the importance of sharing.

Note: One of the purposes of this exercise is to disclaim stereotypes of communities and neighborhoods. Within any community of people are unique talents and stories. Extend the exercise concept into speaking invitations from those you find.

Find Someone Who . . .
exercise one

See how many different names you can collect.

1. Find someone who can describe the beauty of gossamer.

_____

2. Find someone who has rafted on a river.

_____

3. Find someone who can hum a musical selection of Beethoven's.

_____

4. Find someone who has a reptile for a pet.

_____

5. Find someone you never met before.

_____

6. Find someone who would share both a secret and a dream.

_____

Find Someone Who . . .
exercise two

See how many different names you can collect.

1. Find someone who stood close to a rainbow.

_____

2. Find someone with a relative that has celebrated more than ninety birthdays.

_____

3. Find someone who has climbed a mountain.

_____

4. Find someone who collects fossils.

_____

5. Find someone who has traveled in three or more foreign countries.

_____

6. Find someone who writes poetry on his own initiative.

_____

Find Someone Who . . .
exercise three

See how many different names you can collect.

1. Find someone who overcame a handicap.

   _____

2. Find someone who spent more than three consecutive days on the sea.

   _____

3. Find someone whose name appeared in a book.

   _____

4. Find someone who has been aloft in a hot air balloon.

   _____

5. Find someone who has maintained a diary or a journal for more than two years.

   _____

6. Find someone who has spent more than a month in a hospital.

   _____

How is it?————————————

What we perceive are the perceptions of self.

Overview

Without being observed, an item is placed in a paper sack. The group or class task is to determine what is in the sack by asking questions. Questions are asked in a rotating fashion if the group is in a circle or by rows if seated in a traditional classroom setting. Questions are phrased always in the same way: "How is it?" The person responsible for placing the item in the sack responds to each question by citing one of the item's attributes or a personal reaction to the item.

For example, suppose the item in the sack is a photograph of a friend.

First question . . . ."How is it?"
Response . . . ."Friendly!"
Second question . . . ."How is it?"
Response . . . ."Dependable!"
Third question . . . ."How is it?"
Response . . . ."Miniaturized!"

After all group members have asked one "How is it?" question, then a guess is written on paper.

Teaching Suggestions for How is it?

- This game can be played effectively with small groups. Provide two or three rounds of questions per student in groups of less than ten members.

- Consider stimulating this exercise with some items of your own as the game's first responder.

- Encourage students, for future playings, to bring to class items
    - of pride
    - of achievement
    - of special significance
    - of lasting memory
    - of personal meaning

- This game can be academically oriented, as well. Try writing concepts and significant events on paper for placement in the sack.

- The focus of the game should be positive with an atmosphere of acceptance. By playing the game, acceptance is nurtured. Ideally suited for those remaining minutes before the final bell.

Star Power ————————

Overview

Students are to select three behaviors to concentrate on for a full school week. At the end of the week, an attempt is made by all students to determine the individual behaviors chosen by each student.

Teacher Directions

1. Distribute copies of Star Power and Star Power Legend to all students on a Monday.

2. Each student is to select three of five behaviors. The behaviors selected must be exhibited for an entire week at school. Use the Star Power Legend sheet to secretly color three selected behavior boxes. This sheet, upon completion, is not to be shown to other students until Friday.

3. The Star Power Symbol is to be colored with the colors chosen. The Symbol may be taped to a notebook or, if the classroom is self-contained, taped to students' desktops. The Symbol should be seen consistently by all students.

4. The task is to determine, at the end of one school week, what three behaviors each student selected.

5. Distribute copies of the Star Power Score Sheet for ease of determining behaviors on a Friday.

Teaching Suggestions

By placing emphasis on starlike qualities, you give importance to them. Try to extend these behaviors through identification.

- What are the starlike qualities of

    Christ?
    Ghandi?
    Mother Teresa?
    Abraham Lincoln?
    Martin Luther King?
    Ma-ka-tai-me-she-kia-kiak
        or Black Hawk, Chief of the
                        Sauk and Fox?

- What should the starlike qualities be of a

    leader?
    physician?
    parent?
    friend?
    teacher?

- In what ways might starlike qualities make a difference at

    home?
    school?
    work?

Star Power
Symbol

Star Power Legend

☐ Sharing: A willingness to share or offer what I have to others. This may include school materials or information or advice.

☐ Cooperating: A willingness to participate with others. Getting along with others.

☐ Assisting: A willingness to assist and to help others.

☐ Listening: A willingness to really listen to what others are saying. A willingness to ask questions so that what is being said, I will understand.

☐ Supporting: To be a friend. To find ways to show acceptance even if I find disagreement with what is said.

To be done without observation by others:

Select three colors and three behaviors. Color each of the three behaviors a different color. Use these same colors to color each star of your star power symbol.

Perform these three behaviors for the entire week. See if others can decode what behaviors your colors represent.

Do not show this legend to anyone.

Star Power Score Sheet

Scoring Directions

Place x's in three boxes in connection with each name. The x's indicate the behaviors you think each student selected for the week.

Use the Score Sheet during the entire week.

Names	SUPPORTING	LISTENING	ASSISTING	COOPERATING	SHARING

For each name you accurately scored, congratulate those students on their starlike qualities.

Postscript to Star Power

Do not maintain this same exercise over an extended period of time. Do try different behavioral listings using the same format. Behaviors such as courteous, caring, dependable, friendly, gentle, helpful and trustful would be a few to choose from.

So much false reward has been given to children for conforming and achieving in classrooms in recent years. I have seen candy and other rewards given to children for doing the expected. We must, as teachers, bring forth the intrinsic desire among children to be the best they can become. Acknowledging behavior and achievement in positive ways is a beginning. This is the purpose of this exercise.

A house is just a house;
It takes effort to make a house a home.
A classroom is just a room;
It takes effort to make a room a classroom.

A home can make for a better classroom;
A classroom can make for a better home.

Cooperative Components

Overview

Students, in groups of five to six members, will do a mime of a selected machine. Other groups will venture guesses as to the machine being mimed.

Student Directions

- As a group, decide on a machine to be. Also as a group, decide what machine parts to individually perform. Each part performed will be performed in mime. In other words, there will be silence as you perform the functions of the machine. Since a machine is a synthesis of all parts working together, it is important that you work together in a cooperative way. Each group member must be involved as a machine part.

- Possible Possibilities

    - an automatic washing machine
    - a car wash
    - a pinball machine
    - a computer software game
    - an electronic musical keyboard
    - an automatic bowling pin machine

- More Possible Possibilities

    - an automatic garage door
    - a merry-go-round
    - an oscillating fan
    - a hand-held hair dryer
    - a cafeteria dirty dish conveyor system
    - automatic door opener system
    - an elevator
    - a hydraulic automobile jack
    - a motor on a motorboat
    - a soda or candy machine dispenser

Teacher Directions

1. Provide five to ten minutes for group planning.

2. Provide time for group machine presentations.

3. Provide time for guessing.

- Questions

    - In what ways is the holistic working of machine parts like human cooperation?

    - Which is more important—the team planning or the team product?

    - In what ways is a functioning machine like a functioning community? How does a community function? What are the "parts" of a community? In what ways do the "parts" of a community function? In what ways might they malfunction?

Cooperative Inventions

> **Negotiation is an aspect of living.**

Overview

Three teams of students (Teams A, B, and C) are given one page of invention parts. Each page is different for each team. The objective is to paste together an invention that would perform a major cleaning task. The game allows for trading of pieces among the three teams.

Rules

- Each team is allowed one minute to look over all of the invention parts. At this time a different page of the invention parts is given to each team.

- Ten minutes is allowed for team planning and a determination as to what pieces they want to trade and what pieces they want to return. Individual invention pieces are cut out from the page at this time.

- Three minutes for negotiating the first trade.

- Three minutes for individual team planning and the revising of plans, if necessary.

Rules (continued)

- Three minutes for additional trading time.

- Paste together pieces on paper for the invention.

  Penalties:

  - A piece may be taken from a team for violent argumentation. Differences of opinions must be stated with a smile.

  - Bitter complaints may be settled by the declared malfunctioning of an invention.

Teaching Suggestions

1. Designate some students to act as observers to detect high levels of cooperation among teams and among team members. Allow time for positive reactions of cooperation.

2. Discuss how negotiation is often a component of cooperation.

   - What kinds of negotiations are necessary in families? In places of work? In school?

3. Try this exercise again but with different rules. Ask groups to use all three pages of invention parts to piece together in a multi-purpose cleaning invention.

4. Discuss how any new product or invention requires cooperation, such as financial cooperation, cooperation from retail outlets and cooperation from perspective users or buyers.

Team A's Beginning Parts

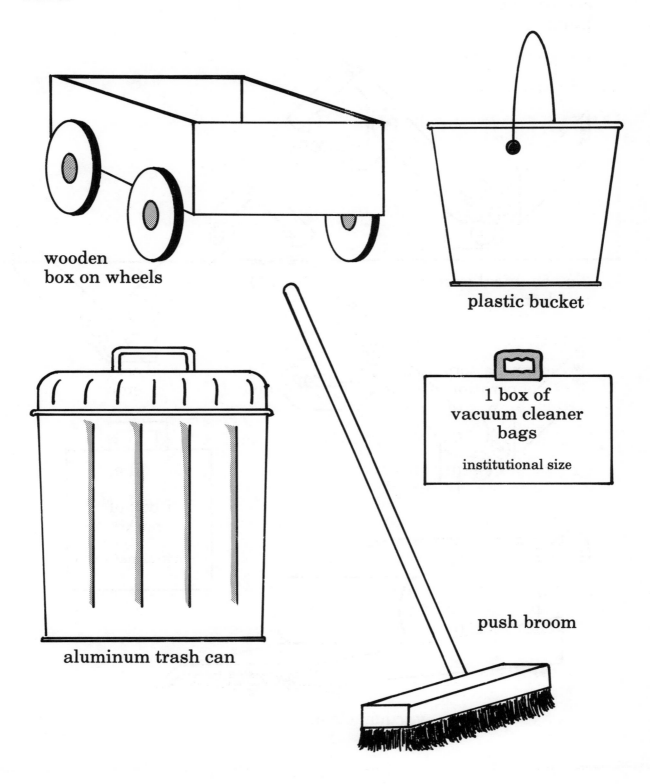

wooden
box on wheels

plastic bucket

aluminum trash can

push broom

1 box of
vacuum cleaner
bags

institutional size

**Team B's
Beginning
Parts**

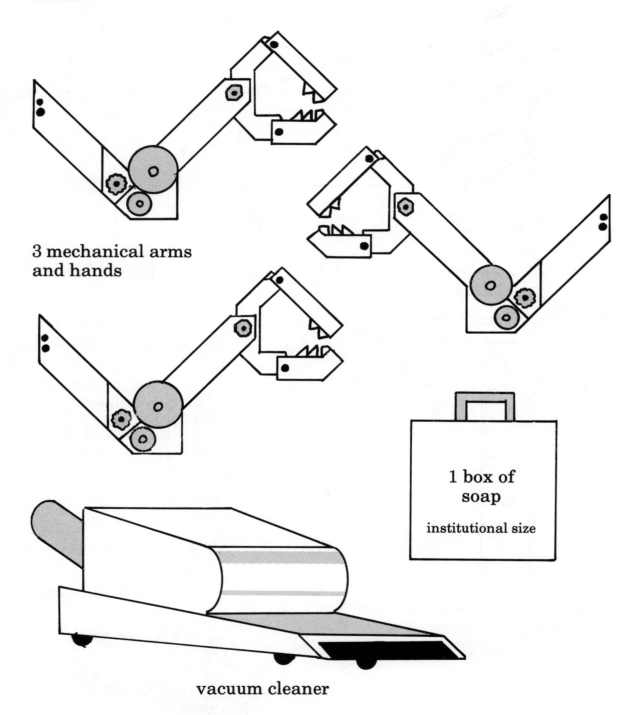

3 mechanical arms
and hands

1 box of
soap

institutional size

vacuum cleaner

**Team C's
Beginning
Parts**

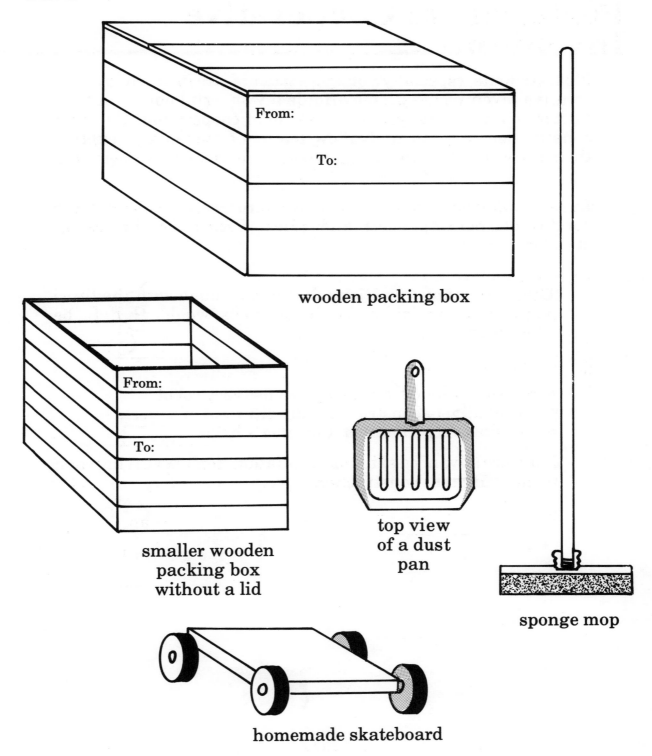

From:

To:

wooden packing box

From:

To:

smaller wooden
packing box
without a lid

top view
of a dust
pan

sponge mop

homemade skateboard

Postscript to Cooperative Inventions

Most students, especially younger students, are inclined towards creative inventiveness. This affords a wonderful opportunity to nurture both creativity and the skills of cooperation. Consider construction projects that allow teams of students to express their inventiveness and to experience the skills of cooperation.

In developing exercises for the above purposes, consider specific conditions, contingencies and rules. Creativity thrives on structure.

There are many variations that can be done with the three pages of invention parts. Some parts would need to be eliminated, but . . .

as teams . . .

* cooperatively construct a pizza delivery robot
* cooperatively construct a baby-sitter robot
* cooperatively construct a teacher's helper

For more advanced skills of negotiation, consider giving each team a different construction topic.

Suggested Readings

Bloom, Benjamin S. *Developing Talent in Young People.* New York: Ballantine Books, 1985.

Canfield, Jack, and Wells, Harold C. *100 Ways to Enhance Self-Concept in a Classroom.* Englewood Cliffs, New Jersey: Prentice-Hall, Inc., 1976.

Clark, Barbara. *Growing Up Gifted.* Columbus, Ohio: Charles E. Merrill Publishing Co., 1983.

Eberle, Bob, and Hall, Rosie Emery. *Affective Direction.* Buffalo, New York: D.O.K. Publishers, Inc., 1979.

_____ . *Affective Education Guidebook.* Buffalo, New York: D.O.K. Publishers, Inc., 1975.

Franck, Frederick. *The Zen of Seeing.* New York: Vintage Books, 1973.

Fromm, Erich. *The Art of Loving.* New York: Harper & Row, 1956.

Harmin, Merrill. *I've Got to Be Me!* Niles, Illinois: Argus Communications, 1976.

_____ . *This Is Me!* Niles, Illinois: Argus Communications, 1978.

Harmin, Merrill, and Sax, Saville. *A Peaceable Classroom: Activities to Free Student Energies.* Minneapolis: Winston Press, 1977.

Houston, Jean. *The Possible Human.* Los Angeles: J.P. Tarcher, 1982.

Jung, Carl G. *Man and His Symbols.* New York: Doubleday, 1969.

Loughmiller, Campbell. *Wilderness Road.* Austin, Texas: The Hogg Foundation for Mental Health, The University of Texas, 1980.

MacKinnon, Donald W. *In Search of Human Effectiveness.* Buffalo, New York: The Creative Education Foundation, Inc., in association with Creative Synergetic Associates, Ltd., 1978.

Maslow, Abraham H. *Motivation and Personality.* 2nd ed. New York: Harper & Row, 1970.

_____ . *Toward a Psychology of Being.* Princeton, New Jersey: D. Van Nostrand Company, 1968.

May, Rollo. *The Courage to Create.* New York: Norton, 1975.

McLuhan, T.C. *Touch the Earth.* New York: Simon & Schuster, Inc., 1971.

Miller, John. *The Compassionate Teacher.* Englewood Cliffs, New Jersey: Prentice-Hall, 1981.

Noller, Ruth B. *Mentoring: A Voiced Scarf.* Buffalo, New York: Bearly Limited, 1982.

Paterson, Katherine. *Bridge to Terabithia.* New York: Avon Books, 1979.

Postman, Neil. *The Disappearance of Childhood.* New York: Harper & Row, 1982.

Raths, Louis E., Harmin, Merrill, and Simon, Sidney B. *Values and Teaching.* rev. ed. Columbus, Ohio: Charles E. Merrill Publishing Co., 1977.

Rogers, Carl R. *On Becoming a Person.* Boston: Houghton Mifflin, 1961.

_____ . *A Way of Being.* Boston: Houghton-Mifflin, 1980.

Saint-Exupery, Antoine de. *The Little Prince.* New York: Harcourt, Brace & World, 1943.

Silverstein, Shel. *The Giving Tree.* New York: Harper, 1964.

Simon, Sidney B., Howe, Leland W., and Kirschenbaum, Howard. *Value Clarification: A Handbook of Practical Strategies for Teachers and Students.* New York: Hart, 1972.

Stanish, Bob. *Lessons from the Hearthstone Traveler.* Carthage, Illinois: Good Apple, Inc., 1988.

_____ . *Mindglow.* Carthage, Illinois: Good Apple, Inc., 1986.

Sturner, William F. *Risking Change.* Buffalo, New York: Bearly Limited, 1987.

Trelease, Jim. *The Read Aloud Handbook.* New York: Penguin Books, 1982.

Torrance, E. Paul, et. al. *Save Tomorrow for the Children.* Buffalo, New York: Bearly Limited, 1987.

Williams, Margery. *The Velveteen Rabbit.* Garden City, New York: Doubleday and Company, Inc., 1968.